FAST

331

I
I
N

R
T

APPA
EDUCATIONAL FOUNDATION

**ROBERT L. GILSTRAP**  **CATHY BIERMAN**  **THOMAS R. MCKNIGHT**

Robert L. Gilstrap is a professor in the Graduate School of Education at George Mason University in Fairfax, Virginia, where he coordinates programs in Middle Education (grades 4-8) and teaches courses in curriculum and instruction and social studies methods for the middle grades. A past president of the Association for Childhood Education International, Gilstrap has written publications for teachers, parents, and early adolescents.

Cathy E. Bierman is a seventh-grade English teacher at Thomas Jefferson Middle School in Arlington, Virginia, and adjunct professor of education at George Mason University. She has worked closely with the teachers in her school, preparing them for the transition to a middle school organization. Bierman received her doctorate in middle school curriculum and instruction from Virginia Polytechnic Institute and State University.

Thomas R. McKnight has taught in the Arlington (Virginia) Public Schools since 1969. Currently he is chairperson of the English department and building computer coordinator at H.B. Woodland School, an alternative school (grades 6-12), which he helped to create.

Series Editor, Derek L. Burleson

# Improving Instruction in Middle Schools

by
Robert L. Gilstrap,
Cathy Bierman,
and
Thomas R. McKnight

Library of Congress Catalog Card Number 92-80138
ISBN 0-87367-331-X
Copyright © 1992 by the Phi Delta Kappa Educational Foundation
Bloomington, Indiana

This fastback is sponsored by the Memphis State University Chapter of Phi Delta Kappa, which made a generous contribution toward publication costs.

The chapter sponsors this fastback in honor of the 67 charter members of the chapter, which was founded on 17 May 1958. The charter members are: Louis Anderson, Thomas Ashcroft, James Atkins, Robert Baker, Woodrow Behannon, Reading Black Jr., James Bowen, Richard Boyce, James Bradberry, Jerry Brillheart Jr., William Brotherton, Edward Brown, W. Day Brown, Ferdinand Byzet Jr., William Carson, Charles Castellow, Robert Clark, Raymond Coltharp, Fred Colvett, Edward Crawford, Walter Danley, William D'Aoust, Earnest Dumas, David Dunbar, Norman Ervin, Irving Filderman, Kinneth Floyd, Jimmie Fortune, George Harris, Walter Helms, Charles Hensley, John Hirschmann Jr., William Hodges, Cecil Humphreys, Austin Jackson, Bryan Koonce, Irl Krause Jr., Theodore Kreh, Robert Lance, John Long, Troy Long, John Midkiff, James Moore, Robert Morgan, John Morrison, Robert Ogle, James Parker, James Pirtle, George Pratt, Franklin Raines, James Raines, Joe Ray, Robert Robison, Alvin Rogers, Lowell Schmid, Carl Self, Leroy Sholly, Billy Smith, William Stephenson, Randall Storms, William Swafford, Chester Tate, Billy Joe Vaughan, Thomas Vison, Hawthorne Wallis, John Winfrey, and Grady Woody.

# Table of Contents

# Introduction

In 1989, when the Carnegie Council's Task Force on the Education of Young Adolescents released its influential report, *Turning Points: Preparing American Youth for the 21st Century*, it made eight recommendations for improving the lives of young people, ages 10 to 15. Four of these recommendations deal specifically with improving instruction in middle grade schools. They are the focus of this fastback.

Since the beginning of the middle school movement in the early 1960s, leaders in the field have emphasized the importance of making instruction developmentally appropriate for the early adolescent. Despite these leaders' pronouncements, the Carnegie Task Force report argues that the education of early adolescents continues to be misguided, amounting to a national crisis. It describes the current scene as a "volatile mismatch between the organization and curriculum of middle grade schools and the intellectual and emotional needs of young adolescents." Evidence of this crisis is found in such indicators as the truancy and dropout rate and the incidence of substance abuse and teenage pregnancy, to name a few.

The purpose of this fastback is to examine the recommendations from *Turning Points* related to middle school instruction and to suggest ways they might be implemented. To do this, we first review earlier efforts at improving instruction for early adolescents and then summarize the recommendations from *Turning Points* related to instruction. This is followed by an overview of the characteristics and needs of the early adolescent. Then we present 10 instructional strategies that we believe are developmentally appropriate for this age group and explain why they are appropriate. Finally, we discuss the organizational setting in which these strategies can best be implemented.

Our hope is that this fastback will be a useful guide for teachers and administrators involved in middle school education as well as for preservice students planning to teach in middle schools. It also will be useful for helping parents understand why particular instructional strategies are used with their middle school children.

# Why Focus on Instruction?

It is significant that the Carnegie Task Force chose to focus on instruction in four of its eight recommendations in *Turning Points*. It is through the instructional program that teachers can have the most direct impact on the lives of early adolescents and can see the immediate results of their efforts. Further, the focus on instruction supports the principle that those most directly involved in the education of early adolescents are the ones who should be making the decisions about what they do. Only in this way can we ensure that instruction is truly appropriate.

Before examining the recommendations in *Turning Points* related to instruction, we provide some historical perspective by looking at some earlier influential statements about the education of early adolescents.

## Earlier Efforts to Improve
## the Education of Early Adolescents

In its 1918 report, *Cardinal Principles of Secondary Education*, the National Education Association's Commission on the Reorganization of Secondary Education recommended a plan "whereby the first six years shall be devoted to elementary education designed to meet the needs of pupils approximately 6 to 12 years of age, and to secondary education designed to meet the needs of pupils approximately

12 to 18 years of age." The commission further recommended that the secondary years "may well be divided into two periods which may be designated as the junior and senior periods."

According to Alexander and George (1981), the junior high school that evolved as a result of the commission's report caught on because of the increasing enrollment following World War I. The moving of two or three grades into a new junior high organization (although not necessarily a new building) was supported by many educators, who saw it as a practical and economical way of dealing with the enrollment problem. Further, it was a way of responding to the criticisms of G. Stanley Hall and other developmental psychologists, who were calling for a different type of school organization that would better meet the needs of this age group.

By the early 1960s the junior high school structure was being criticized for not meeting the needs of the early adolescents. They were too much like "little" high schools, said the critics. The time was right for looking at a new organizational plan, and this occurred in 1963 at a conference on the junior high school held at Cornell University. There William M. Alexander presented a proposal for reorganizing schools serving early adolescents, which he called "a middle school" (Wiles and Bondi 1981).

Several schools represented at the conference were already doing many of the things being proposed, and they became good prototypes. By 1980, according to Alexander and George (1981), there were 5,000 middle schools in operation compared to not more than 100 in 1960. In 1982, the National Middle School Association (NMSA) released *This We Believe*, a position paper describing the essential ingredients of a true middle school. By 1990, according to NMSA, 25% of all public school buildings were designated as middle schools (grades 5-8, 6-8, 6-7, or 7-8), and about 40% of the students in the seventh grade attended middle schools.

Yet, despite the rapid growth of middle schools as an organizational structure, the authors of *Turning Points* found it necessary to state: "Middle grade schools — junior high, intermediate, and middle schools — are potentially society's most powerful force to recapture millions of youths adrift and help young people thrive during early adolescence. Yet all too often these schools exacerbate the problems of young adolescents." What should be done?

## Recommendations of the Carnegie Task Force on Adolescent Development

In preparing its report to the nation, the Task Force commissioned papers; interviewed experts in relevant fields; met with teachers, principals, health professionals, and leaders of youth-serving organizations; and examined firsthand promising new approaches for educating young adolescents. Integrating current research with the professional judgment of innovative middle school educators, the Task Force made eight recommendations for improving the education of early adolescents, four of which deal with instruction.

1. *Create small communities for learning.* Too many early adolescents are lost in the large schools, especially those in some urban settings. As a result, their intellectual and emotional needs go unmet. A school should be a place where close, trusting relationships with adults and peers create a community conducive to personal growth and intellectual development.

Schools in which the enrollment exceeds 1,000 should be organized into schools-within-a-school or houses, creating communities of students and teachers who work together as teams and small-group advisories, thus ensuring that every student is known well by at least one adult.

Every student should be assigned an adult advisor. These advisors would most likely be teachers, but that does not mean that teachers would replace guidance counselors. Guidance counselors would continue to play a central role by assisting advisors in developing group activities for the advisory period, by consulting with advisors on students' problems, by counseling students with problems that go be-

11

yond an advisor's area of competency, and by linking students to appropriate community agencies when the school cannot adequately meet their needs.

2. *Teach a core academic program.* Although states and school districts mandate broad curriculum outlines, each middle school faculty should have the authority to develop a full academic program for all students that integrates English, mathematics, science, social studies, foreign languages, and fine arts.

The curriculum in most schools covers all these subject areas, but it often lacks depth. Students learn bits and pieces of information but are not asked to see relationships across disciplines, to do higher-order thinking, or to apply what they learn by solving problems. To improve curriculum and instruction for middle grades, we should be teaching young adolescents: 1) to think critically, 2) to develop healthful lifestyles, 3) to be active citizens, 4) to integrate subject matter across disciplines, and 5) to learn how to learn as well as how to take tests successfully.

In the transformed middle school, tests will more closely resemble real learning tasks. State and national achievement tests will differ from current practice. One promising alternative assessment is the use of portfolios containing samples of students' work. With this alternative, assessment would be linked more closely with ongoing classroom activities.

3. *Ensure success for all students.* Regardless of achievement level or the pace at which they learn, all students should be able to succeed in the basic core curriculum. To ensure that all students learn will require: 1) grouping students according to their interests and learning needs, 2) using flexible class scheduling to maximize learning, and 3) expanding the kinds of opportunities for learning.

Rather than rigidly grouping or tracking students by ability levels in separate classes, grouping arrangements should be fluid, changing on the basis of student needs and interests or on the nature of the learning task. This might involve using such proven approaches as cooperative learning and cross-age tutoring. By using varied groupings and having flexible class scheduling, teacher teams will have larger blocks of instructional time for cross-disciplinary learning projects.

The middle school should be structured to provide for a variety of learning opportunities that nourish the strengths and overcome the weaknesses of individual students. Such a structure would allow additional support for students needing more time to learn as well as for students to demonstrate excellence, thus gaining confidence and personal satisfaction by becoming very good at something. Such a structure will require new institutional arrangements with new roles for teachers and administrators, necessitating negotiations with the teacher union in some cases.

4. *Empower teachers and administrators to make instructional decisions*. Decisions affecting the learning experiences of middle grade students should be made by those closest to them and who know them best. By empowering staff at the building level, students will feel they are living and working in a responsive environment in which they have defined rights and clear responsibilities. Empowering staff will help to create a middle grade school that produces responsible and ethical citizens, who will be active participants in the community. To achieve empowerment will require: 1) giving teachers greater authority for decisions affecting classroom operations, 2) establishing building governance committees, and 3) designating teacher leaders to guide the learning process.

The empowered middle school staff would be organized into teacher teams with the authority for: 1) deciding how curricular goals are to be achieved, 2) selecting and allocating funds for instructional materials, 3) identifying and developing interdisciplinary curriculum themes, 4) scheduling classes, 5) planning field experiences, and 6) evaluating student performance. With such authority, the teacher team would be directly accountable for student performance.

In addition to teacher teams for each school-within-a-school or house, there should be a building governance committee made up of representatives from each house, administrators, support staff, parents, students, and representatives from the community. This committee strives to reach decisions by consensus on matters affecting the whole school and serves in an advisory capacity to the building principal. The building principal would be responsible for the safe and efficient functioning of the entire school and for creating a positive climate for each house to carry out its program.

Within the house structure, there would need to be a staff person to serve as the leader for each teacher team. This person would have some administrative duties but would spend most of the time working with the team on developing curriculum, obtaining needed resources, helping solve problems with individual students, and offering assistance when additional support services are needed. Both the house leader and building principal will need considerably more freedom to make decisions than middle school administrators currently have. At both levels of leadership, these individuals will have a key role in shaping the learning experiences of young adolescents.

To understand the implications of these four recommendations summarized above, we now need to look at the characteristics and developmental needs of this age group.

# What Do We Know About the Early Adolescent?

*This We Believe* (1982), a position statement from the National Middle School Association (NMSA), states that "the middle school concept is the embodiment of valid educational ideals, ones that emerge from the nature and needs of the age group to be served, and that those ideals provide clear direction for the needed educational programs." It goes on to say that the middle school movement is "founded in these realities of human development and the allied principles of learning." So what are the "realities of human development" in early adolescents?

For starters, there is not even agreement among human development specialists on a term to describe this age group. Terms commonly used in the literature include early adolescent, young adolescent, emerging adolescent, pre-adolescent, late childhood, and transescent. For consistency in this fastback we will use the term, early adolescent.

Early adolescence is generally considered to fall in the age range of 10 to 14. But if we use the onset of puberty as a criterion, it can occur earlier or later than these ages. However, the vast majority of those we call early adolescents fall within grades five through eight.

Because of the wide variations in the rate of physical maturation and the resulting anxiety it creates among students who are early or late maturers, NMSA believes that early adolescents should be grouped by developmental age rather than by the rigid chronological age-graded system, which has dominated U.S. education since 1860. Developmental age means readiness for learning based on specific characteristics of the learner, irrespective of chronological age. Youngsters at the same developmental age may range from two to three years in chronological age.

## Developmental Characteristics and Needs

Although each early adolescent is unique, there are some characteristics that appear to be common.

Physical characteristics:
- rapid body growth
- sexual maturation
- change in level of physical activity

Social and emotional characteristics:
- need for strong self-esteem
- need for understanding self and feelings
- need for autonomy and independence
- concern about body image

Intellectual characteristics:
- gradual shift from concrete to early formal reasoning
- varied learning styles
- distractability and short attention span
- broad interests but often short-lived and unfocused
- present-time orientation

Middle school teachers must take into account these common characteristics when planning curriculum and devising instructional methods. At the same time, they must recognize that skill and achievement levels of this age group fall along a broad continuum. Some students will demonstrate rapid progress and then experience plateaus or even regression. According to Lipsitz (1984), at the "root of the difficulty in schools for young adolescents are massive individual differences in their development." To serve these individual differences requires varied instructional methods, such as committee work and simulations for those who need much peer interaction or independent study for those who have the ability to assume responsibility for their own learning.

In her study of successful schools for early adolescents, Lipsitz (1984) identified seven categories of needs that these schools addressed in their structure and programs:

1. competence and achievement
2. self-exploration and definition
3. social interaction with peers and adults
4. physical activity
5. meaningful participation in school and community
6. routine, limits, and structure
7. diversity

These needs are supported by Johnston (1985) in his study of 10 middle schools identified as exemplary. To these needs, Van Hoose and Strahan (1988) have added:

8. opportunities to explore concepts and generate ideas from concrete experiences
9. opportunities to explore values and decision-making

In the next chapter, we will discuss several instructional strategies that we believe are developmentally appropriate and address the above needs of early adolescents.

# Instructional Strategies for Early Adolescents

In this chapter, we describe 10 instructional strategies that we believe to be developmentally appropriate and that can be implemented by educators who have been empowered to make instructional decisions, regardless of the organizational structure of the school in which they work. We present these strategies in the form of vignettes based on the literature and on our observations and experiences in middle schools in northern Virginia. Following each vignette, we discuss how developmental needs are being met through use of the strategy.

## Learning Centers

In this sixth-grade class, the language arts/social studies teacher uses learning centers for part of his instructional program. He has identified several objectives in the curriculum that lend themselves to the learning center approach, which takes into consideration students' needs, interests, and abilities. One learning center focuses on a specific skill, another on presenting information, and a third on encouraging students to use their creativity. As we enter the classroom, several students have finished their assigned seat work and are now ready to go to the learning centers, which are located in three separate areas of the classroom out of heavy traffic patterns.

One boy is working at the skills center, which focuses on improving handwriting. There is a Peanuts poster on a bulletin board showing Charlie Brown writing a letter to the girl with red hair. The catchy title for this center is "Write Your Heart Out, Charlie Brown!" Materials at the center include handwriting samples to copy, a letter-formation chart, paper, and pencils. Instructions for the student are printed on a chart mounted on the wall over the table where the student works. They say: 1) pick a writing sample, 2) copy what's on the sample on your paper, 3) do three different letters to finish the center. (All of the samples are love letters from Charlie Brown.) The student is asked to evaluate his skill by comparing his writing with the writing sample and to check it against the letter-formation chart. There is a pocket on the chart for completed papers. On the pocket is a class roster. When the boy finishes his paper, he places it in the pocket and checks off his name.

In the information learning center, titled "Learning About the Incas," another student is reading the directions listed on a cardboard poster that sits on a table in the corner of the room. On the table is a film-strip viewer/cassette player ready for students to use. The directions are: 1) put on earphones, 2) turn on filmstrip and cassette player, 3) look and listen, 4) summarize what you have learned in your social studies learning log.

The third center features a large poster of Garfield the cat saying, "Express Yourself." It has a cardboard box covered with bright construction paper containing assorted colored papers and other odds and ends to use for making a collage. The box sits on top of a bookcase along with glue and scissors. The students are asked to construct a collage that expresses their feeling about a Shel Silverstein poem found in one of the poetry collections in the bookcase.

*Why are learning centers developmentally appropriate?* One of the developmental needs mentioned in the last chapter is the need for diversity. For this age group, the classroom must be a place that offers a variety of ways to achieve curriculum objectives. Learning centers are a simple way to supplement regular instruction. By using colorful and eye-catching displays that appeal to students' interests, learning centers allow students to work independently and at their own pace on a variety of curriculum-related tasks. Middle school students can even assist in setting up learning centers, which relieves the burden on the busy teacher.

## Cooperative Learning

Activity 1. When we enter this seventh-grade language arts classroom, one of the first things we notice is that the teacher has organized her class into cooperative learning groups of four to five students. The teacher is giving a dramatic reading of Edgar Allen Poe's "The Tell-Tale Heart." The pupils enjoy being read to and are attentive throughout.

After reading the story, the teacher asks members of each group to count off so that each student has a number of 1 to 4 or 5. Then she gives them a question and asks all students to write out an individual answer to the question before discussing it with their group. In their groups the students must come to an agreement on the answer to the question. She then calls out a number and the student with that number reports the answer the group has agreed on. This strategy is called "Numbered-Heads Together."

The teacher's first question is: "Do you believe that the narrator is a madman? Why or why not?" The students work for about five minutes writing out their individual answers and then discuss them in their cooperative learning groups, with the goal of reaching consensus on an answer they can share with the rest of the class. For this first question, the teacher calls on the number 3 in each group to respond. For the second question, she might ask the number 4 to respond, and so on. By the end of the period, each member of the group has had an opportunity to report to the total class with the support of his or her group. And since the students did not know which number the teacher would call, all had to be ready to respond with their group's answer if their number was called.

Activity 2. In this seventh-grade social studies classroom, the students have been studying the Civil War. They are now meeting in cooperative learning groups to pull together everything they have learned in preparation for writing a final report. In the groups, the students record all the pertinent information on large sheets of newsprint and then post the sheets on the wall. Some of the groups have several sheets of material.

Then the students move around the room reading all of the information and ideas generated by the other groups. (This activity is called "Gallery" because the students walk around the room as if they were in an art gallery.) Occasionally the teacher reminds the students to keep moving and not to spend all their time reading the ideas of just one group.

After reading all the information generated by the groups, the students return to their desks to do individual writing assignments as a final activity. The assignment is to be in the form of a letter to President Abraham Lincoln, written as if the students were historical or fictional characters from the period they have been studying. When the letters are completed, the teacher plans to dress up as Lincoln; and the students will pretend they are meeting with him to read their letters aloud and defend their viewpoints on some aspect of the Civil War about which they feel strongly.

*Why is cooperative learning developmentally appropriate?* These two activities, developed by Kagan (1985), capture the essence of the cooperative learning approach, because all students are involved and learning from each other. In the first activity, each group's answer could be written on the board, thus allowing the teacher and students to make comparisons among group responses and to see how much agreement there is among them. This total class discussion provides the interaction with peers needed by early adolescents as well as opportunities to gain confidence by speaking out and defending their answers before their peers. In the second activity, students are also learning from each other and have an opportunity to respond creatively by writing a letter defending their position from the viewpoint of a historical character.

## Cross-Age Tutoring

In this eighth-grade class, students are conferencing in pairs in preparation for tutoring sixth-graders in writing. Before today's session, the teacher has met with the sixth-grade teacher to find out in what specific areas her students need help. In addition, he has worked with the class on such matters as establishing rapport with the younger students, using questions that require the sixth-graders to think and do the work themselves, and focusing first on their development and organization before dealing with mechanics such as punctuation and spelling. Today the eighth-graders are practicing their tutoring techniques on each other. Working in pairs, they practice asking each other the same questions and using the same techniques that they will use with the sixth-graders later in the week. The teacher circulates, listening to and observing what is essentially a peer-tutoring activity. At the end of the session, the class discusses what worked and what did not work. The students then write an entry in their journal about the session. The teacher reminds the class that there will be group sharing and journal writing after they have tutored the sixth-graders so they can improve the next time they try cross-age tutoring.

*Why is cross-age tutoring developmentally appropriate?* This experience satisfies early adolescents' developmental need for feelings of competence and achievement. Their involvement in cross-age tutoring requires them to articulate what good writing is; and by helping younger students to write better, they become better writers themselves. Although this example from Reigstad and McAndrews (1984) focused on writing instruction, cross-age tutoring can be used in all core curriculum areas.

## Interdisciplinary Units

In this school seventh-grade teachers of the core subjects of English, science, math, and social studies make up interdisciplinary teams. Each team works with the same group of students and has a common period for planning instruction. Team members also have one period daily for individual planning time. In the daily team planning meeting, the special education teachers join the group. The assistant principal also attends regularly. Daily planning meetings facilitate the development of interdisciplinary units. The teachers can plan what they will be doing related to the unit in each of their classes and then can evaluate progress in meeting their established goals.

Every seventh-grader is required to do a science project; and if the students choose to do so, they may enter their project in the county science fair. The science project is accompanied by a research paper describing the entire process that the students went through in developing the project and its conclusions. The science teacher worked with the English teacher in the initial planning for this unit and involved the math and social studies teachers as well. The English teacher began this interdisciplinary unit by teaching the seventh-graders the research skills needed for carrying out the science project and for writing the research paper. She first reviewed the library skills needed to find the most current information about particular science topics. For example, she spent time on how to use the *Readers' Guide to Periodical Literature*. After the students had gathered information on their topics, they spent several weeks with the science teacher organizing their data for their science projects.

When the students were ready to write their papers describing their science projects, the English teacher guided them in developing an outline. The math teacher assisted those who needed help with mathematical calculations or with graphs and tables to illustrate what they had learned. In developing their conclusions, the students had to use thinking skills that had been emphasized in their social studies classes, so that teacher spent some class time helping students with that part of their paper.

*Why are interdisciplinary units developmentally appropriate?* Because all members of the interdisciplinary team were helping them, the students in this school learned science and research skills, which gave them the confidence to write a research paper. Since everyone did a science project, this was not an activity restricted to the science "stars" at the school. The team wanted everyone to succeed and to feel like a winner, without any pressure to enter the project in the county science fair. All students were able to explore their individual interests in science and to demonstrate that they had the competence to carry out a project and write a research paper.

## Learning Activity Packages

In this sixth-grade math/science classroom, the teacher is individualizing instruction by using learning activity packages she has developed herself. Each package contains materials designed to teach mathematical concepts in the sixth-grade curriculum. She developed the packages based on student needs revealed in diagnostic tests given earlier in the school year. She explains to the students that they can contract to do as many learning packages as they want, that they have so much time to do each package, and that they must work on the package independently.

As the students open their packages, you can see that they all contain manipulatives designed to teach particular mathematical concepts in a concrete way. In addition, each package contains a pre-assessment test, a list of objectives to be accomplished, a series of instructional activities to reach these objectives, and a post-assessment test. Some of the packages contain follow-up activities for students who need additional work. When all packages have been distributed, the teacher moves about the room working with individual children as needed, providing feedback, and recording progress.

*Why are learning activity packages developmentally appropriate?* Early adolescents need to explore concepts using concrete experiences. Having students contract to use learning activity packages gives them hands-on experiences in math and is an excellent way of individualizing instruction. It also provides diversity in their instruction.

## Independent Study

In this eighth-grade class, some of the students are conferring with the teacher about their independent study projects. Their project topics, selected with the teacher's guidance, are ones the students want to pursue in depth over a specified period of time. The teacher helps the students develop a plan for carrying out their project, including setting deadlines for accomplishing various parts of the project. An important aspect of planning is helping the students to structure their time.

After the students and the teacher have agreed on a topic and a plan, the teacher confers with each student on a regular basis according to the schedule established to check progress and to offer guidance if needed. As the project nears completion, the teacher has a final conference to review the study and to schedule a time for sharing the project with the class.

On this day, one of the students is reporting on her independent study, which involved reading Shakespeare's *Romeo and Juliet* and comparing it with the film version of the play and with the musical, *West Side Story*, which is based loosely on the play. The focus of her report was on the similarities and differences between the original play and its contemporary versions in different media.

*Why is independent study developmentally appropriate?* Early adolescents need time to explore their own interests, which may not be a part of the regular curriculum. However, students at this age need some structure to carry out an independent study project successfully. Many need guidance in organizing their time if the project extends over several weeks. Also, the opportunity to share the project with the class certainly contributes to their feelings of self-worth and competence.

# Group Investigation

In this seventh-grade classroom, the language arts teacher wants her students to read several classic young adult novels and is using a group investigation strategy to get students to work together. To match students in randomly selected pairs, she puts two slips of paper for each author into a jack-o-lantern, called the "Jolly Pumpkin," she keeps on her desk. On one slip of paper is the first name of the author and on the second slip the last name. Each student reaches into the "Jolly Pumpkin" and draws out a slip. Their partner for the group investigation is the student who draws the slip with the matching first or last name of the author. The teacher tells them they cannot switch names, because she wants them to work with somebody they have not worked with before.

After the students are matched in pairs and know what author they will be reading, the teacher takes the entire class to the library, where the librarian has prepared a display of at least two novels for each of the authors to be read. The students were told before going to the library that they were expected to read at least two novels by the author they drew. Each of the students in a pair will read the same two books and then collaborate in writing a report about the books and the author. They also can read another book by the same author for extra credit.

After the students have checked out their books, the teacher asks if they have any questions about the group investigation activity. One student asks how much time he and his partner will have to read the two books and write their report. She responds that they will have two weeks to read each book and then another week to write their report, using an outline that she will provide. She adds that some class time can be used for reading, but most of it must be done as homework. However, the writing of the report will be done in class. The teacher explains that she will be checking with each pair regularly to see how they are progressing. She emphasizes that each member of the pair has equal responsibility for carrying out the group investigation.

*Why is group investigation developmentally appropriate?* Group investigation provides for the early adolescent's need for positive experiences with their peers. To respond to their need for limits and structure, the teacher in the vignette above provided them with a time frame and an outline for their final report. She also reminded them that there would be regular progress checks along the way in order to help them keep on schedule. Carrying out a successful group investigation serves students' need for a sense of competence and achievement. The skills learned in this activity could be transferred to more complex group investigations.

## Simulations

In this eighth-grade, social studies/language arts classroom, the students are involved in a simulation using the commercial package, *Gateway*. In this simulation, the students take on the role of an immigrant who came to the United States around the turn of the century. Prior to doing the simulation, the students have studied about U.S. immigration in their textbook and have written papers on "The Old Country," "The Crossing," and other topics related to the U.S. immigration experience. They also have engaged in some heated discussions about why some people were accepted and others excluded.

On this day, the class is involved in a simulation, which is the culminating activity for the unit. Some of the students are playing the role of immigration officers at Ellis Island who are assigned to different stations that the immigrants must pass through (loyalty, immigrant papers, background, vocation, health, and character). Other students take the role of immigrants. They are encouraged to try to speak the foreign language they are currently studying mixed with halting English. Some of the students actually are newcomers to the United States, so they can speak the language they use at home with their parents.

The roles of the immigration officers and the immigrants are fully described in the *Gateway* materials. Those students assigned to be immigrants can assume the role of someone from their own family who was an immigrant, or they can select a role from a list of immigrant names provided in the simulation materials. They all wear ID cards tied around their necks giving information about the immigrant they are role playing.

The students are then told to go to each of the six stations in any order. If there is a long line at one station, they go to another. If they finish early, they are encouraged to stay in character and talk with each other. Students at the loyalty station are asked to take an oath to prove their loyalty to the United States. At the health station they answer questions about diseases and other health problems. At the vocation station they must discuss their future work plans and whether or not they have the promise of a job. At the background station they are asked questions about their reasons for immigrating. At the character station they are answering questions related to any trouble they might have had with the law. And at the immigrant paper station they are checked to make sure they have all the proper paperwork.

The classroom scene is active and lively as the students apply what they have learned in their immigrant studies. The teacher supervises the activity to ensure that students carry out the role playing according to the directions in the simulation, but for the most part the students do the simulation on their own. Afterward, the teacher conducts a debriefing session where the students discuss what they learned and how they might make the next simulation even more successful.

*Why are simulations developmentally appropriate?* Simulations serve many of the developmental needs of middle school students. They provide for interaction with peers and allow students of different ability to work together on a common project. They engage students in physical activity and give them an opportunity to try out different roles, which help them to understand themselves better. Because simulations are different, they help meet the early adolescent's need for diversity. Many simulations provide concrete experiences that help students to understand complex concepts, and they provide opportunities for exploring values and decision-making.

## Discovery Approach

A group of sixth-graders has just returned to class after having collected leaves in their glorious fall colors that have fallen from trees on their middle school campus. Their math/science teacher asks them to spread out the leaves on their desks. Then, using an overhead, he projects a list of questions to guide the students as they examine their leaves. Several magnifying glasses are available for those who want to examine their leaves in greater detail.

The students work in pairs and try to discover all they can about different kinds of leaves. Then they record their findings in a learning log that each student maintains. As the students work, the teacher moves around the room offering help to those who need it as they record their data. After about 20 minutes, the teacher asks the students to share some of their discoveries about leaves with the class. Several do so, reading information they have entered in the learning logs. Before the class ends, the teacher hands out large envelopes for storing the leaves until the next time the class meets, when they will continue sharing what they have learned.

*Why is the discovery approach developmentally appropriate?* Middle school students need concrete experiences in order to gain information and explore concepts. The discovery approach serves this need, especially in math and science, since many middle school students lose interest in these subjects during the transition from elementary to high school. The activity described in the vignette above took the students out of the classroom and put them in the role of active learners, thus providing diversity in their learning.

## Using Microcomputers

This class of 28 seventh-graders is on its way to the computer lab to do some writing. They already have some familiarity with using the computer from a previous session in the lab, when they wrote cinquains in connection with a poetry unit. In that session the students learned the structure of the cinquain, practiced writing some on the computer, and learned how to use the copy command.

As the students enter the lab, they pick up a disk and a handout and go with a partner to their computer stations. The handout covers points the students learned in their previous session in the computer lab. For today's session the teacher has three goals: learning about word choice, learning a new computer command, and practicing cooperative behaviors. By limiting her instructional goals, the teacher is able to have a short conference with each pair of students.

The students discuss what they want to write about on the computer, using a list of topics they had brainstormed the day before. The teacher leads a discussion about word choice; a few students are even consulting a thesaurus. Soon after they begin writing on the computer, a pair of students wave their hands frantically, indicating they want help. They have forgotten the "copy" command. "Ask three, then ask me," the teacher reminds them. This is a cooperative learning technique the teacher uses to get students to help each other before asking for the teacher's help. As the session draws to a close, the students make a final save, print out their work, hand it in, and return their disks. Then the teacher gives the class a writing assignment for their next session: "If you could invent a new key for the computer, what would it make the computer do? What would you name it?" This assignment is intended to stimulate students' creativity regarding new uses of computer technology.

*Why is using microcomputers developmentally appropriate?* The microcomputer is a learning tool that can be used to accomplish a variety of middle school curriculum objectives. Using their computer skills to write on topics of their own choosing gives early adolescents a sense of competence and achievement. In the vignette above, the students engaged in brainstorming and worked in pairs at the computer terminal, thus providing for peer interaction and cooperative learning. The assignment to think and write about new uses for the computer challenges students to be imaginative.

# Organizing Middle Schools
# to Serve Developmental Needs

In the previous two chapters, we have reviewed the characteristics and developmental needs of early adolescents and have described 10 instructional strategies that we believe can be used to meet those needs. We also endorse the recommendations in *Turning Points* regarding instruction for middle school students. They are: 1) create small communities for learning, 2) teach a core academic program, 3) ensure success for all students, and 4) empower teachers and administrators to make instructional decisions.

In this final chapter, we offer our recommendations on how middle schools should be organized to serve the developmental needs of early adolescents. These recommendations are based on the experiences of the two teachers who helped write this fastback, both of whom work in schools that exemplify what we are recommending.

Their schools are organized into groups of approximately 200 pupils, who are taught by interdisciplinary teams. We believe that the interdisciplinary team is the key to developing a true community of learning. Because the teams meet regularly and work with a manageable number of students, they are able to plan instructional strategies that are developmentally appropriate for early adolescents. In addition to team planning time, teachers have a daily time for individual planning or to meet with students for whom they serve as advisors. The teams consist of core subject teachers (English, math, science, and social studies) and special education teachers. The assistant principal serves as liaison between the teams and the principal.

This organizational structure works because teachers and principals are empowered to make instructional decisions and to evaluate the effectiveness of the instructional program, which is in keeping with the recommendation of the Carnegie Task Force in *Turning Points*.

Throughout this fastback, we have emphasized the importance of teachers and principals being actively involved in transforming their schools into communities of learning. It is our hope that readers of this fastback will find our recommendations helpful in designing developmentally appropriate instructional strategies that allow early adolescents to thrive in middle schools.

# References

Alexander, W.M., and George, P.S. *The Exemplary Middle School.* New York: Holt, Rinehart and Winston, 1981.

Carnegie Council on Adolescent Development. *Turning Points: Preparing American Youth for the 21st Century.* New York: Carnegie Corporation of New York, 1989.

Epstein, J.L., and MacIver, D.J. *Education in the Middle Grades.* Columbus, Ohio: National Middle School Association, 1990.

Gilstrap, R.L., and Martin, W.R. *Current Strategies for Teachers: A Resource for Personalizing Instruction.* Glenview, Ill.: Scott, Foresman, 1975.

Hilke, E.V. *Cooperative Learning.* Fastback 299. Bloomington, Ind.: Phi Delta Kappa Educational Foundation, 1990.

Johnston, H.J., with de Perez, J.M.R. "Four Climates of Effective Middle Schools." In *Schools in the Middle.* Reston, Va.: National Association of Secondary School Principals, 1985.

Kagan, S. *Cooperative Learning: Resources for Teachers.* Riverside: University of California-Riverside, 1985.

Lipsitz, J. *Successful Schools for Young Adolescents.* New Brunswick, N.J.: Transaction Books, 1984.

National Education Association, Commission on the Reorganization of Secondary Education. *Cardinal Principles of Secondary Education.* U.S Bureau of Education, Bulletin 35. Washington, D.C.: U.S. Government Printing Office, 1918.

National Middle School Association. *This We Believe.* Columbus, Ohio, 1982.

Mack, J. *Gateway*. Lakeside, Calif.: Interact, n.d.

Reigstad, T.J., and McAndrews, D.A. *Training Tutors for Writing Conferences*. Urbana, Ill.: ERIC, NCATE, 1984.

Van Hoose, J., and Strahan, D. *Young Adolescent Development and School Practices: Promoting Harmony*. Columbus, Ohio: National Middle School Association, 1988.

Virginia Department of Education. *Framework for Education in the Middle School Grades*. Richmond, Va., 1990.

Wiles, J., and Bondi, J. *The Essential Middle School*. Columbus, Ohio: Charles E. Merrill, 1981.

# Fastback Titles *(Continued from back cover)*

# PDK Fastback Series Titles

(Continued on inside back cover)